German Christmas Cookbook

© Copyright 2018. Laura Sommers.
All rights reserved.
No part of this book may be reproduced in any form or by any electronic or mechanical means without written permission of the author. All text, illustrations and design are the exclusive property of Laura Sommers

Introduction	1
Almond Spritz Cookies	2
German Sauerbraten	3
Authentic German Potato Salad	4
Boiled Potatoes	5
German Beef Rouladen	6
German Christmas Stollen	7
German Sausage Stuffing	9
German Vegetable Stuffing	10
German Apple Stuffing	11
German Christmas Cookies	12
German Plum Cake	13
German Apple Cake	14
German Apple Dapple Cake	15
German Apple Pudding Cake	16
Zwetschekuchen (German Plum Tart)	17
German Lemon Cake	18
German Marble Cake	19
German Chocolate Chip Pound Cake	20
German Chocolate Cake Frosting	21
German Chocolate Cake	22
German Turkey	24
German Pancakes	25

German Potato Pancakes 26
German Spaetzle Dumplings 27
Gurkensalat (German Cucumber Salad).......................28
German Chocolate Fudge 29
German Gingerbread Hearts Lebkuchen.....................30
Gingerbread Cookies (Nuernberger Lebkuchen) 32
Austrian Linzer Cookie...34
Pfeffernüsse (German Iced Gingerbread Cookies) 35
German Almond Paste Cookies 37
German Caraway Bread 38
German Chocolate Fudge 39
Krautkrapfen (Bavarian Kraut Crullers).......................40
German Bremer Klaben Holiday Bread 41
German gingerbread Men Cookies 42
German Egg Noodles 43
German Sweet Potato Pie 44
German Chocolate Glazed Peaches 45
German Chocolate Cherry Cheesecake 46
German Butter Cookies..47
Almond-Filled Stollen..48
Prime Rib With Fresh Herb Sauce.................................50
German Mulled Wine 52
German Kraut And Keilbasa 53
German Bratwurst Supper...54

Slow-Cooked German Sauerkraut Soup 55
German Hazelnut Yule Log Cookies 56
German Potato Dumplings 57
German Lentil Soup 58
Pfannkuchen (German Filled Pancakes) 59
Chocolate Lebkuchen (Gingerbread Cookies) 60
Gingerbread Men Cookies 62
German Eggnog 63
German Red Cabbage 64
German Snow Angel Cookies 65
Pork Schnitzel With Dill Sauce 66
German Parmesan Baked Potatoes 67
German Cranberry Conserve 68
German Sauerkraut Casserole 69
Bavarian Pot Roast 70
Roast Christmas Goose 71
Zimtsterne 72
Pfeffernuesse Cookies 73
German Potato Dumplings 74
Kummelweck Rolls 75
Hasenpfeffer (Rabbit Stew) 76
German Potato Plum Dumplings 77
Angel's Braid (Engelszopf) 79
Christmas Gingerbread House 80

About the Author 82
Other Books by Laura Sommers 83

Introduction

Christmas is an extremely popular holiday in Germany, beginning with Advent four weeks before Christmas Day. Advent calendars, St. Nicholas Day and Krampus Night are some of the holiday rituals commonly practiced. Germany has an old fashioned Christmas feel which lasts most of December.

Christmas in Germany include such traditional foods as Duck, Goose, Gingerbread, Stollen (the German version of Fruitcake) and cookies. Lots and lots of cookies.

If you love the tradition of Christmas feasts and traditional foods, you will want to try all these wonderfully delicious German Christmas recipes and not just during the holidays.

Almond Spritz Cookies

Ingredients:

1 cup butter, softened
1/2 cup sugar
1/2 cup packed brown sugar
1 egg
1/2 tsp. almond extract
1/2 tsp. vanilla extract
2-1/2 cups all-purpose flour
1/4 tsp. baking soda
1/4 tsp. salt

Directions:

1. Green and red colored sugar, chopped candied cherries and red frosting, optional
2. In a mixing bowl, cream butter and sugars.
3. Beat in egg and extracts.
4. Combine flour, baking soda and salt; gradually add to the creamed mixture.
5. Using a cookie press fitted with the disk of your choice, press dough 2 in. apart onto ungreased baking sheets.
6. Sprinkle with colored sugar if desired.
7. Bake at 375° for 7-9 minutes or until edges just begin to brown.
8. Immediately add cherries if desired, lightly pressing onto cookies.
9. Cool on wire racks. Decorate with frosting if desired.

German Sauerbraten

Ingredients:

3 pounds beef rump roast
2 large onions, chopped
1 cup red wine vinegar, or to taste
1 cup water
1 tbsp. salt
1 tbsp. ground black pepper
1 tbsp. white sugar
10 whole cloves, or more to taste
2 bay leaves, or more to taste
2 tbsps. all-purpose flour
Salt and ground black pepper to taste
2 tbsps. vegetable oil
10 gingersnap cookies, crumbled

Directions:

1. Place beef rump roast, onions, vinegar, water, 1 tbsp. salt, 1 tbsp. black pepper, sugar, cloves, and bay leaves in a large pot.
2. Cover and refrigerate for 2 to 3 days, turning meat daily.
3. Remove meat from marinade and pat dry with paper towels, reserving marinade.
4. Season flour to taste with salt and black pepper in a large bowl.
5. Sprinkle flour mixture over beef.
6. Heat vegetable oil in a large Dutch oven or pot over medium heat.
7. Cook beef until brown on all sides, about 10 minutes.
8. Pour reserved marinade over beef, cover, and reduce heat to medium-low.
9. Simmer until beef is tender, 3 1/2 to 4 hours. Remove beef to a platter and slice.
10. Strain solids from remaining liquid and continue cooking over medium heat.
11. Add gingersnap cookies and simmer until gravy is thickened about 10 minutes.
12. Serve gravy over sliced beef.

Authentic German Potato Salad

Ingredients:

3 cups diced peeled potatoes
4 slices bacon
1 small onion, diced
1/4 cup white vinegar
2 tbsps. water
3 tbsps. white sugar
1 tsp. salt
1/8 tsp. ground black pepper
1 tbsp. chopped fresh parsley

Directions:

1. Place the potatoes into a pot, and fill with enough water to cover.
2. Bring to a boil, and cook for about 10 minutes, or until easily pierced with a fork.
3. Drain, and set aside to cool.
4. Place the bacon in a large deep skillet over medium-high heat.
5. Fry until browned and crisp, turning as needed. Remove from the pan and set aside.
6. Add onion to the bacon grease, and cook over medium heat until browned.
7. Add the vinegar, water, sugar, salt and pepper to the pan.
8. Bring to a boil, then add the potatoes and parsley.
9. Crumble in half of the bacon.
10. Heat through, then transfer to a serving dish.
11. Crumble the remaining bacon over the top, and serve warm.

Boiled Potatoes

Ingredients:

2 1/4 pounds medium yellow-flesh potatoes (such as Yukon gold)
1 pinch salt
1/3 cup chopped fresh parsley

Directions:

1. Place potatoes in a large pot and cover with salted water.
2. Bring to a boil.
3. Reduce heat to medium-low and simmer until tender, about 20 minutes.
4. Drain.
5. Sprinkle on parsley and serve hot.

German Beef Rouladen

Ingredients:

1/4 cup Dijon mustard
8 (4 oz.) pieces round steak, pounded 1/4 inch thick
1/2 cup minced onion
2 tsps. paprika
2 tsps. salt
2 tsps. freshly ground black pepper
8 slices bacon
3 tbsps. canola oil
1 (12 oz.) can beef broth
1 1/4 cups water
2 tbsps. cornstarch
1 cup warm water
1/4 cup sour cream

Directions:

1. Spread 1/2 tbsp. mustard over one side of each piece of meat.
2. Sprinkle the onion, paprika, salt, and pepper evenly over the steaks.
3. Lay one slice of bacon on each piece.
4. Roll the steaks jelly-roll style and secure with toothpicks.
5. Heat the canola oil in a skillet over medium heat.
6. Cook meat on all sides until browned.
7. Add the beef broth and water; bring to a boil.
8. Reduce heat to medium low; cover and simmer until tender, about 30 minutes.
9. Remove the meat rolls. Strain the broth mixture and return liquid to the skillet.
10. Whisk together the cornstarch and 1 cup of water.
11. Slowly pour the cornstarch slurry into the skillet, stirring continually until the sauce has thickened, 2 to 3 minutes.
12. Stir in the sour cream.
13. Return rolls to the sauce.

German Christmas Stollen

Traditional German fruitcake

Ingredients:

1-3/4 cups chopped mixed candied fruit
1/2 cup plus 2 tbsps. rum, divided
2 pkgs. (1/4 oz. each) active dry yeast
1/2 cup warm water (110 degrees F to 115 degrees F)
1-1/2 cups warm 2% milk (110° to 115°)
1-1/4 cups butter, softened
2/3 cup sugar
2-1/2 tsps. salt
2 tsps. grated lemon peel
1 tsp. almond extract
7 to 8 cups all-purpose flour
4 eggs
1/3 cup slivered almonds
1 can (8 oz.) almond paste
1 egg yolk
2 tsps. water
2 to 2-1/4 cups confectioners' sugar

Directions:

1. In a small bowl, combine candied fruits and 1/2 cup rum; let stand, covered, 1 hour.
2. In a small bowl, dissolve yeast in warm water.
3. In a large bowl, combine milk, butter, sugar, salt, lemon peel, almond extract, remaining rum, yeast mixture and 4 cups flour.
4. Beat on medium speed until smooth. Cover with plastic wrap and let stand in a warm place, about 30 minutes.
5. Beat in eggs.
6. Stir in enough remaining flour to form a soft dough (dough will be sticky).
7. Drain candied fruit, reserving rum for glaze. Reserve 1/2 cup candied fruit for topping. Stir almonds and remaining candied fruit into dough.
8. Turn dough onto a floured surface; knead until smooth and elastic, about 6-8 minutes. Place in a greased bowl, turning once to grease the top.
9. Cover with plastic wrap and let rise in a warm place until doubled, about 1 hour.
10. Punch down dough; divide into three portions.
11. On a greased baking sheet, roll each portion into a 12-in. circle.
12. Crumble one-third of the almond paste over one-half of each circle.

13. Fold dough partially in half, covering filling and placing top layer within 1 in. of bottom edge.
14. Cover with kitchen towels and let rise in a warm place until doubled in size, about 1 hour. Preheat oven to 375 degrees F.
15. In a small bowl, whisk egg yolk and water; brush over loaves.
16. Bake 30-35 minutes or until golden brown.
17. Cover loosely with foil if tops brown too quickly.
18. Remove from pans to wire racks to cool completely.
19. In a small bowl, mix reserved rum with enough confectioner's sugar to make a thin glaze. Drizzle over stollen.
20. Sprinkle with reserved candied fruit.

German Sausage Stuffing

Ingredients:

1 lb. ground round
1 lb. pork sausage
6 stalks of celery, chopped
1 onion, chopped
1 lb. mushrooms, sliced
2 eggs
1/2 tsp. thyme
2 tsp. ground sage or to taste
1 can evaporated milk
1 pkg. stuffing mix

Directions:

1. Brown meat.
2. Drain well.
3. Sauté in butter or steam celery, onion and mushrooms.
4. Beat eggs and add milk and vegetables.
5. Combine all together with stuffing mix and seasonings.
6. Add broth to moisten.
7. Bake in a greased and uncovered casserole for 1 hour at 325 degrees F.

German Vegetable Stuffing

Ingredients:

2 cup green peppers
2 cup celery
2 cup mushrooms
2 cup onions
1/2 box saltines, grated very fine
1 lb. butter
Salt and pepper to taste

Directions:

1. Chop all ingredients very small.
2. Put all in large frying pan with butter and cook until soft and little gold, about 20 minutes. open, no cover.
3. Remove from heat.
4. Add saltines. Very fine like cracker meal and mix well.
5. Stuff turkey, chicken, peppers, or use as hors d'oeuvres on crackers.

German Apple Stuffing

Ingredients:

1 loaf day old white bread
1/3 cup butter
1 medium size (1/2 cup) onion, chopped
1/2 cup chopped celery
1/4 cup chopped celery leaves
2 tbsp. chopped parsley
Salt and pepper to taste
2 c. milk
2 eggs, lightly beaten
5 cups Red Delicious apples, pared, cored, and chopped
1/4 cup raisins
1 tbsp. of sage
1/2 tbsp. of thyme

Directions:

1. Combine all ingredients in large bowl.
2. Add milk to moisten.
3. Bake in a greased and uncovered casserole for 1 hour at 325 degrees F.

German Christmas Cookies

Ingredients:

8 eggs
4 cups sugar
4 oz. chopped citron
4 oz. blanched almonds, chopped
grated rind of 2 lemons
9 cups flour
1/2 tsp. ground cloves
2 tsp. nutmeg
1/4 tsp. black pepper

Directions:

1. In a large bowl, beat eggs.
2. Add sugar and beat until smooth, about 15 minutes.
3. Add citron, almonds, and lemon rind.
4. Sift together flour.
5. Add ground cloves, nutmeg, and black pepper to flour and sift again.
6. Add to the first mixture.
7. Roll out dough 3/4 inch thick.
8. Cut into small rounds 1-inch in diameter.
9. Before baking, turn each cookie upside down, put a drop of water on each and bake at 350 degrees F. for 15 minutes.

German Plum Cake

Cake Ingredients:

1 cup white sugar
1/4 cup butter, softened
2 eggs
2 cups all-purpose flour
2 tsps. baking powder
25 plums, pitted and halved

Crumble Topping Ingredients:

2 cups brown sugar
2 cups all-purpose flour
1/2 cup cold butter, cut into cubes

Directions:

1. Preheat oven to 350 degrees F (175 degrees C).
2. Grease a 9x13-inch baking dish.
3. Beat white sugar, softened butter, and eggs together in a bowl until creamy.
4. Whisk 2 cups flour and baking powder together in another bowl. And flour mixture to butter mixture and stir until just combined.
5. Press mixture into the bottom of the prepared baking dish.
6. Arrange plums on top of butter mixture in the baking dish.
7. Stir brown sugar, 2 cups flour, and 1/2 cup cold butter together in a bowl until mixture resembles coarse crumbs.
8. Spread crumble mixture over plums in the baking dish.
9. Bake in the preheated oven until cake is set and plums are soft, about 1 hour 30 minutes.
10. Cool for 1 hour before slicing.

German Apple Cake

Ingredients:

2 eggs
1 cup vegetable oil
2 cups white sugar
2 cups all-purpose flour
1 tsp. baking soda
2 tsps. ground cinnamon
1 tsp. salt
1 tsp. vanilla extract
4 cups apples, peeled, cored and diced
1/2 cup chopped walnuts
2 (3 oz.) packages cream cheese
3 tbsps. butter, softened
1 1/2 cups confectioners' sugar
1 tsp. vanilla extract

Directions:

1. Preheat oven to 350 degrees F (175 degrees C).
2. Grease and flour a 9x13 inch pan. In a medium bowl, mix together flour, baking soda, cinnamon and salt. Set aside.
3. In a large bowl, combine eggs, oil and sugar. Beat until foamy.
4. Add flour mixture and beat well.
5. Add vanilla and stir in chopped apples and walnuts.
6. Pour into a 9x13 inch pan.
7. Bake for 45 to 50 minutes, or until a toothpick inserted into the cake comes out clean.
8. Allow cake to cool, then spread with cream cheese frosting.
9. To make the frosting:
10. In a medium bowl, combine cream cheese, softened butter, confectioners sugar and 1 tsp. vanilla.
11. Beat until smooth, then spread on cake.

German Apple Dapple Cake

Ingredients:

1 1/2 cups vegetable oil
3 eggs
1 cup packed brown sugar
2 tsps. vanilla extract
1 tsp. baking soda
1 tsp. salt
3 cups all-purpose flour
1 cup chopped walnuts
4 cups chopped apples
1 cup packed brown sugar
1/2 cup butter
1/4 cup heavy whipping cream

Directions:

1. Preheat oven to 350 degrees F (175 degrees C).
2. Grease and flour a 9x13 inch pan, or a 10 inch tube pan.
3. Stir the flour, baking soda and salt together and set aside.
4. In a large bowl, cream the oil, eggs, 1 cup brown sugar and 2 tsps. vanilla.
5. Add the flour mixture and mix well. Stir in the chopped apples and nuts.
6. Pour batter into prepared pan.
7. Bake at 350 degrees F (175 degrees C) for 30 minutes, or until a toothpick inserted into the center of the cake comes out clean.

Topping Directions:

1. In a saucepan, combine 1 cup brown sugar, 1/2 cup butter and 1/4 cup cream.
2. Bring to a boil and continue boiling for 3 minutes.
3. Cool slightly and pour over warm cake.

German Apple Pudding Cake

Ingredients:

2 cups apple, peeled, cored, and chopped
1 cup white sugar
1 egg 1 tsp. vanilla extract
1 cup all-purpose flour
1 tsp. baking soda
1 1/2 tsps. ground cinnamon
3/4 cup chopped walnuts
3/4 cup raisins
1/2 cup brown sugar
1/2 cup white sugar
2 tbsps. all-purpose flour
1 cup water
1/2 cup butter
1 tsp. vanilla extract
1/2 cup chopped walnuts
1/2 cup raisins

Directions:

1. Preheat oven to 350 degrees F (175 degrees C).
2. Grease and flour an 8 inch square pan.
3. In a large bowl, mix apples and sugar together.
4. Let stand until sugar is thoroughly dissolved, about 8 minutes.
5. Stir egg and vanilla into apple mixture.
6. Sift together flour, baking soda and cinnamon; stir into apple mixture.
7. Fold in nuts and raisins. Pour batter into prepared pan.
8. Bake in the preheated oven for 40 to 45 minutes, or until a toothpick inserted into the center of the cake comes out clean.
9. Pour topping over cake while cake is still hot.
10. For the Topping: In a saucepan, combine 1/2 cup brown sugar, 1/2 cup white sugar and 2 tbsps. flour.
11. Stir in the water.
12. Cook over medium heat, stirring, until mixture boils and thickens. Remove from heat and stir in butter, vanilla, chopped walnuts and raisins.
13. Stir until butter melts, then pour over cake.

Zwetschekuchen (German Plum Tart)

Ingredients:

4 cups all-purpose flour
1 1/3 cups white sugar
1 tsp. grated fresh lemon peel
1 pinch ground cinnamon
1 cup butter, cut into chunks
2 eggs
2 egg yolks
1 tsp. water, if needed
3 pounds Italian prune plums
1 tbsp. white sugar

Directions:

1. Place the flour, 1 1/3 cup of sugar, lemon peel, cinnamon, and butter into the work bowl of a food processor, and process until the mixture turns grainy.
2. Stop the machine, add eggs and egg yolks, and process in the machine until the mixture gathers itself up into one dough ball.
3. If the dough doesn't ball up, stop the machine, sprinkle several drops of water onto the dough, and process again.
4. Place the dough into a covered container and refrigerate at least 3 hours or preferably overnight.
5. The next day, preheat oven to 350 degrees F (175 degrees C).
6. Allow the dough to rest at room temperature for about 30 minutes to warm up.
7. Roll out the dough on a well-floured surface to make a 9 1/2-inch circle.
8. Dough will be rich and sticky.
9. Scrape up the dough circle, and press into a 9-inch pie dish.
10. Quarter and slice the plums, and place skin sides down onto the dough in a neat ring, starting at the outer edge and working in a neat row towards the center.
11. Bake in the preheated oven until the plums are bubbling hot and the crust starts to brown, about 45 minutes.
12. Allow the tart to cool, and sprinkle with 1 tbsp. of sugar before serving.

German Lemon Cake

Ingredients:

1 1/8 cups butter, softened
1 1/4 cups white sugar
5 eggs
3 tbsps. rum (optional)
1 cup all-purpose flour
1 cup cornstarch
1/3 cup lemon juice
1 cup confectioners' sugar

Directions:

1. Preheat the oven to 350 degrees (175 degrees C).
2. Grease a 9x5 inch loaf pan.
3. In a large bowl, beat the butter and sugar together until light and fluffy.
4. Beat in the eggs, one at a time, mixing well after each one.
5. Stir in the rum, then mix in the flour and cornstarch.
6. Pour into the prepared loaf pan.
7. Bake for 1 hour and 15 minutes in the preheated oven, or until a knife inserted into the crown comes out clean.
8. Cool for at least 10 minutes before removing from the pan.
9. While the cake is baking, mix together the lemon juice and confectioners' sugar.
10. When the cake comes out of the oven, poke with a long fork or knitting needle all over.
11. Pour the glaze over the top and let it soak in.
12. Cut into slices to serve.

German Marble Cake

Ingredients:

1 cup butter
1 1/2 cups white sugar
4 eggs
1 cup milk
1 tsp. almond extract
3 1/4 cups all-purpose flour
1 tbsp. baking powder
1/8 tsp. salt
1/4 cup unsweetened cocoa powder
3 tbsps. dark rum

Directions:

1. Preheat oven to 350 degrees F (175 degrees C).
2. Grease and flour one 10 inch tube pan.
3. In a large bowl, cream the butter with the sugar.
4. Beat in the eggs, then the milk and almond extract.
5. In another bowl, stir together the flour, baking powder and salt.
6. Beat the flour mixture into the creamed mixture.
7. Turn half of the batter into another bowl and stir in the cocoa and rum.
8. Layer the light and dark batters by large spoonfuls and then swirl slightly with a knife.
9. Bake the cake in at 350 degree F (175 degree C) for about 70 minutes, or until it tests done with a toothpick.
10. Transfer to a rack to cool.

German Chocolate Chip Pound Cake

Ingredients:

2 cups white sugar
1 cup shortening
4 eggs
2 tsps. vanilla extract
2 tsps. butter flavored extract
1 cup buttermilk
3 cups all-purpose flour, sifted
1/2 tsp. baking soda
1 tsp. salt
2 cups German sweet chocolate chips

Directions:

1. Preheat oven to 300 degrees F (150 degrees C).
2. Grease and flour 2 - 9 inch loaf pans.
3. Sift flour, baking soda and salt together and set aside.
4. In a large bowl, cream shortening and sugar until light and fluffy.
5. Beat in the eggs one at a time, then stir in the vanilla and butter flavoring.
6. Add the flour mixture, alternating with the buttermilk, and mix well. Finally, stir in the chocolate chips.
7. Divide batter into 2 - 9 inch loaf pans.
8. Bake at 300 degrees F (150 degrees C) for 1 hour and 30 minutes, or until a toothpick inserted into the center of cake comes out clean.

German Chocolate Cake Frosting

Ingredients:

1 cup evaporated milk
1 cup white sugar
3 egg yolk, beaten with
1 tsp. water
1/2 cup margarine
1 tsp. vanilla extract
1 cup chopped pecans
1 cup flaked coconut

Directions:

1. In a large saucepan combine evaporated milk, sugar, egg yolks, margarine and vanilla.
2. Cook over low heat, stirring constantly, until thick.
3. Remove from heat and stir in pecans and coconut.
4. Spread on cake while still warm.

German Chocolate Cake

Ingredients:

1/2 cup water
4 (1 oz.) squares German sweet chocolate
1 cup butter, softened
2 cups white sugar
4 egg yolks
1 tsp. vanilla extract
1 cup buttermilk
2 1/2 cups cake flour
1 tsp. baking soda
1/2 tsp. salt
4 egg whites
1 cup white sugar
1 cup evaporated milk
1/2 cup butter
3 egg yolks, beaten
1 1/3 cups flaked coconut
1 cup chopped pecans
1 tsp. vanilla extract
1/2 tsp. shortening
1 (1 oz.) square semisweet chocolate

Directions:

1. Preheat oven to 350 degrees F (175 degrees C).
2. Grease and flour 3 - 9 inch round pans. Sift together the flour, baking soda and salt.
3. Set aside. In a small saucepan, heat water and 4 oz. chocolate until melted.
4. Remove from heat and allow to cool.
5. In a large bowl, cream 1 cup butter and 2 cups sugar until light and fluffy. Beat in 4 egg yolks one at a time.
6. Blend in the melted chocolate mixture and vanilla.
7. Beat in the flour mixture alternately with the buttermilk, mixing just until incorporated.
8. In a large glass or metal mixing bowl, beat egg whites until stiff peaks form. Fold 1/3 of the whites into the batter, then quickly fold in remaining whites until no streaks remain.
9. Pour into 3 - 9 inch pans
10. Bake in the preheated oven for 30 minutes, or until a toothpick inserted into the center of the cake comes out clean.
11. Allow to cool for 10 minutes in the pan, then turn out onto wire rack.
12. To make the Filling:

13. In a saucepan combine 1 cup sugar, evaporated milk, 1/2 cup butter, and 3 egg yolks.
14. Cook over low heat, stirring constantly until thickened.
15. Remove from heat.
16. Stir in coconut, pecans and vanilla.
17. Cool until thick enough to spread.
18. Spread filling between layers and on top of cake.
19. In a small saucepan, melt shortening and 1 oz. of chocolate.
20. Stir until smooth and drizzle down the sides of the cake.

German Turkey

Ingredients:

1 (18 lb.) whole turkey, neck and giblets removed
1 med. onion, peeled
1 large carrot, peeled
1 stalk celery
1 apple, stem removed
1 orange
1/4 cup vegetable oil
1 tsp. salt
1 tbsp. coarsely ground black pepper
1 tsp. soul food seasoning
1 pound sliced smoked bacon
1 turkey sized oven bag

Directions:

1. Preheat the oven to 350 degrees F (175 degrees C).
2. Rinse the turkey, pat dry and place in a large roasting pan.
3. Insert the onion, carrot, and celery into the cavity of the bird.
4. Poke holes in the apple and orange so they will release their juices, and stuff them into the bird.
5. You may have to cut some things in half to get them all inside.
6. Spread oil all over the outside of the bird, and season with salt, pepper and soul food seasoning.
7. Place the turkey into an oven bag, and set back into the pan with the breast facing up. Lay strips of bacon over the entire top.
8. Close the bag.
9. Roast the turkey for about 4 hours, or until the internal temperature reaches 180 degrees F (82 degrees C) when taken in the thickest part of the thigh.
10. Let the turkey rest for 10 or 15 minutes before carving, and use the drippings in your favorite gravy recipe.

German Pancakes

Ingredients:

1/4 cup butter
1 cup all-purpose flour
1 cup milk
6 eggs, lightly beaten
1/8 tsp. salt

Directions:

1. Preheat oven to 350 degrees F (175 degrees C).
2. Melt butter in a medium baking dish.
3. In a medium bowl, mix flour, milk, eggs and salt.
4. Pour the mixture into the prepared baking dish.
5. Bake on center rack in the preheated oven for 30 to 40 minutes, until golden brown.

German Potato Pancakes

Ingredients:

2 eggs
2 tbsps. all-purpose flour
1/4 tsp. baking powder
1/2 tsp. salt
1/4 tsp. pepper
6 medium potatoes, peeled and shredded
1/2 cup finely chopped onion
1/4 cup vegetable oil

Directions:

1. In a large bowl, beat together eggs, flour, baking powder, salt, and pepper.
2. Mix in potatoes and onion.
3. Heat oil in a large skillet over medium heat.
4. In batches, drop heaping tablespoonfuls of the potato mixture into the skillet.
5. Press to flatten.
6. Cook about 3 minutes on each side, until browned and crisp.
7. Drain on paper towels.

German Spaetzle Dumplings

Ingredients:

1 cup all-purpose flour
1/4 cup milk
2 eggs
1/2 tsp. ground nutmeg
1 pinch freshly ground white pepper
1/2 tsp. salt
1 gallon hot water
2 tbsps. butter
2 tbsps. chopped fresh parsley

Directions:

1. Mix together flour, salt, white pepper, and nutmeg.
2. Beat eggs well, and add alternately with the milk to the dry ingredients.
3. Mix until smooth.
4. Press dough through spaetzle maker, or a large holed sieve or metal grater.
5. Drop a few at a time into simmering liquid.
6. Cook 5 to 8 minutes.
7. Drain well.
8. Sauté cooked spaetzle in butter or margarine.
9. Sprinkle chopped fresh parsley on top, and serve.

Gurkensalat (German Cucumber Salad)

Ingredients:

2 large cucumbers, sliced thin
1/2 onion, sliced thin
1 tsp. salt
1/2 cup sour cream
2 tbsps. white sugar
2 tbsps. white vinegar
1 tsp. dried dill
1 tsp. dried parsley
1 tsp. paprika

Directions:

1. Spread cucumbers and onion on a platter.
2. Season with salt and let rest for 30 minutes.
3. Squeeze excess moisture from cucumbers.
4. Stir sour cream, sugar, vinegar, dill, and parsley together in a large bowl.
5. Fold cucumber and onion slices into the sour cream mixture.
6. Refrigerate 8 hours to over night.
7. Garnish with paprika to serve.

German Chocolate Fudge

2 cups semisweet chocolate chips
12 (1 oz.) squares German sweet chocolate
1 (7 oz.) jar marshmallow creme
4 1/2 cups white sugar
2 tbsps. butter
1 (12 fluid oz.) can evaporated milk
1/8 tsp. salt
2 cups chopped pecans

Directions:

1. Combine chocolate chips, German sweet chocolate and marshmallow creme in large bowl.
2. Combine sugar, butter, evaporated milk and salt in heavy skillet.
3. Bring to a boil over medium heat.
4. Cook for 6 minutes, stirring constantly.
5. Pour hot syrup over chocolate mixture.
6. Stir with wooden spoon until smooth. Stir in pecans.
7. Spread into buttered 10x15 inch pan.
8. Let stand until firm.
9. Cut into squares.

German Gingerbread Hearts Lebkuchen

Ingredients:

7 tbsps. butter
3/4 cup honey
5/8 cup sugar
2 1/2 tbsps. cocoa powder
1 tbsp. gingerbread spice mix
5 cups flour
1 1/2 tsp. single- or double-acting baking powder
1/4 tsp. salt
1 egg

Dough Directions:

1. Bring the butter, honey, sugar, cocoa powder and gingerbread spice mix to a boil in a medium-size saucepan.
2. Boil for several minutes until the sugar dissolves, then remove from heat and cool slightly.
3. Sift the flour with the baking powder and salt into a bowl.
4. Make a depression in the bowl and add the egg, then pour the honey mixture over the flour and mix on low speed until a ball of dough can be formed.
5. The ball of dough might still be shaggy but will form a smooth dough as it cools down, so do not add extra flour.
6. Wrap the ball of dough in plastic wrap and put in a safe place at room temperature for 4 to 48 hours.
7. Let dough rest overnight before baking for best results.

Cookie Directions:

1. Heat the oven to 350 degrees F.
2. Roll out half the dough to 1/2-inch thickness on a lightly floured board.
3. Use a large, heart-shaped cookie cutter or your own template to cut out large, heart shaped cookies.
4. If you want to hang these hearts from a ribbon, create one or two holes about 3/4-inch below the rim of the cookie before you bake it.
5. Repeat with the rest of cookie dough. This dough does not re-roll well, so take care to roll it into the right size the first time.
6. Place the cookies on a parchment-lined cookie sheet and bake 20 to 25 minutes, or until the cookies are set in the middle and lightly browned on the bottom.
7. Bake the trimmed scraps to use for practice decorating.

8. Let the cookies cool completely on the baking sheet.
9. They will harden as they cool. Although they are edible, this dough is most often used to make decorative cookies that are hung on the wall or around the recipient's neck and are seldom eaten.
10. Use tinted royal icing to decorate the cookies. You only need about half of the recipe, but you will want to practice decorating with your baked scraps, and you might want to use several colors, so make the whole batch.
11. Tint some of the icing in a separate bowl using normal food coloring. if the icing is not completely tinted you can create swirls of lighter and darker colors as you pipe it.
12. Place the icing in a decorator bag with a leaf tip attached to make the border.
13. Use a writing tip for the words. Find out more about filling and using pastry bags here.
14. Decorate as you like.
15. It is traditional in Germany to write cute sayings in the center and give the cookies to people you like.

Gingerbread Cookies (Nuernberger Lebkuchen)

Ingredients:

1/2 cup butter (softened)
1 cup sugar
4 large eggs
3 cups all-purpose flour
1/2 tbsp. cinnamon, ground
1/2 tsp. cloves, ground
1/8 tsp. allspice, ground
1/16 tsp. nutmeg, ground
1/8 tsp. coriander, ground
1/8 tsp. cardamom, ground
1/8 tsp. ginger, ground
1/8 tsp. anise seed, ground
2 tbsps. cocoa powder
1 1/2 tsps. baking powder (double-acting)
1 cup/225 milliliters milk
1 3/4 cups ground almonds
1/2 cup candied lemon peel, chopped
1 tbsp. rum (or orange liqueur)
1/2 cup raisins, soaked in rum and chopped
1/4 cup coconut (shredded)
32 oblaten (baking wafers, 3-inch size)
1/2 cup granulated sugar
1/4 cup water
1/2 tsp. vanilla
1 to 2 tbsps. rum
1/2 cup confectioners sugar

Directions:

1. Heat oven to 375 degrees F.
2. Cream butter, 1 cup sugar, and eggs until light and fluffy.
3. Mix in flour, spices, cocoa powder, and baking powder, alternating with milk.
4. Note that you can use prepared lebkuchen spices (1 tbsp.) if available rather than the listed spices.
5. Fold in nuts and lemon peel. Stir in rum. Stir in raisins and coconut.
6. Place the oblaten on parchment-lined baking sheets. Drop about 3 tbsps. cookie dough onto the wafer and smooth to the edges.
7. If you are not using the oblaten, draw 3-inch diameter circles on parchment paper using a cup or biscuit cutter as a template.

8. Drop about 3 tbsps. cookie dough into the center of each circle.
9. In both cases, use the back of a spoon to fill out each circle, slightly mounding the dough toward the center.
10. Bake for 15 to 20 minutes.
11. Turn down oven to 350 degrees F if cookies are browning too much.
12. Let cool for a few minutes, then remove to a cookie or cake rack.

Glaze Directions:

1. While the cookies are baking, make the glaze.
2. The glaze is to be applied while the cookies are still warm.
3. Place 1/2 cup sugar and water in a small saucepan on the stove.
4. Bring to a boil and boil for a few minutes.
5. Add vanilla and 1 to 2 tbsps. rum or liqueur. Sift confectioners' sugar over hot sugar syrup and stir.
6. Using a pastry brush, brush warm glaze over warm cookies. Let dry completely.
7. Dry glazed cookies for a day (so the cookie stays a bit crunchy) then store in an airtight container or freeze.

Austrian Linzer Cookie

4 oz. butter (room-temperature)
3/4 cup confectioners' sugar
1/4 tsp. orange extract
1 cup flour all-purpose flour
1/2 cup marmalade (or jam-- raspberry, red currant, plum or apricot)
Garnish: confectioners' sugar for dusting

Directions:

1. In a medium bowl, cream together 4 oz. room-temperature butter, 3/4 cup confectioners' sugar and 1/4 tsp. of either orange or vanilla extract.
2. Stir 1 cup all-purpose flour into the creamed ingredients and knead just until mixture forms a ball.
3. Wrap in plastic and refrigerate for 30 minutes (or up to several days).
4. Heat oven to 350 degrees F.
5. Line a cookie sheet(s) with parchment paper.
6. Dust work surface with confectioners' sugar and roll out cookie dough to about 1/8 inch/3 mm thick.
7. Using a Linzer cookie cutter, cut an even number of bottoms (without the cutout) and an even number of tops (with a hole in the middle). Transfer with a spatula to the prepared cookie sheet(s).
8. If the dough sticks to the work surface too much, roll it out between two pieces of waxed paper or parchment paper or silicone mats.
9. If the dough is too crumbly, warm it a bit. If you need to, you can knead a little bit of water into the dough to make it easier to work with.
10. Bake for 10 to 12 minutes.
11. Remove from oven. Let cool on cookie pans for 5 minutes.
12. Then remove to wire racks to cool completely.
13. To assemble the cookies:
14. Sift confectioners' sugar over the cooled cookie tops (the ones with a hole) and set aside.
15. Spread the bottom half of the cooled cookies with 1 tsp. jam of choice (do not use jelly).
16. Immediately place a dusted cookie top on the jam-coated bottom cookie and press lightly to adhere.

Pfeffernüsse (German Iced Gingerbread Cookies)

Ingredients:

2 1/4 cup all-purpose flour
1/2 tsp. baking soda
1/4 tsp. salt
2 tsps. Lebkuchengewürz (German gingerbread spice blend)
1/4 tsp. finely ground white pepper
1/4 cup ground almonds/almond meal
1/2 cup packed brown sugar
1/3 cup pure honey
5 tbsps. unsalted butter
3 tbsps. heavy cream
1 large egg

Glaze Ingredients:

2 1/2 cups powdered sugar
4 tbsps. hot water

Directions:

1. In a small bowl, combine the flour, baking soda, salt, Lebkuchengewuerz, white pepper and almond meal.
2. Set aside.
3. Combine the brown sugar, honey, butter, and cream in a medium saucepan and heat, stirring frequently, until melted and the sugar is dissolved.
4. Remove from heat and let sit 5 minutes. Stir in the flour mixture.
5. Once incorporated stir in the egg until thoroughly combined. The dough will have a nice glossy sheen.
6. It will be very sticky and that's how it should be.
7. Turn the mixture out onto some plastic wrap and wrap the dough tightly.
8. Refrigerate overnight or for up to two days.
9. Preheat the oven to 350 degrees F.
10. Remove the dough from the plastic wrap and immediately roll it into two strands, each 3/4 inch thick.
11. Slice the rolls into 3/4 inch thick rounds and roll each round into a ball (each ball should be about 3/4 inch large).
12. Work quickly while the dough is still chilled.
13. Place the cookie balls on a line cookie sheet and bake for 15 minutes or until golden brown. Remove and let the cookies cool completely.

14. To make the glaze, combine the powdered sugar and water until smooth.
15. Dip each cookie in the glaze, letting the excess drip off, and place them on a wire rack positioned over a cookie sheet (to catch the drips) and let them sit until the glaze is fully hardened.

German Almond Paste Cookies

Ingredients:

1 lb. sweet almonds
1/4 lb. almond paste
1-1/4 lb. confectioners' sugar
2 egg whites

Directions:

1. Blanch almonds and dry overnight.
2. Next morning, grind them very fine and mix in 1/4 pound almond paste.
3. Add 1-1/4 pounds confectioners' sugar, mix and knead to a stiff paste with egg whites, unbeaten. Put through pastry tube onto cookie sheet.
4. Bake 15 minutes at 325 degrees F.

German Caraway Bread

Ingredients:

2 cups milk, scalded
2 tbsp. sugar
2 tbsp. butter
1 tsp. salt
1 pkg. active dry yeast
1/2 cup lukewarm water plus 1/2 tsp. sugar
2 tbsp. caraway seeds
6 cups rye flour
1 1/2 cups stone ground wheat flour
2 tbsp. vital wheat gluten (optional)

Directions:

1. Dissolve yeast in lukewarm water (110 degrees F) with a 1/2 tsp. sugar.
2. In a saucepan, scald milk (cook until tiny bubbles form around the edges - do not boil).
3. Remove from heat.
4. Add 2 tbsp. sugar, butter and salt to milk.
5. When scalded milk mixture is lukewarm, add yeast and stir to dissolve. Add caraway seeds and rye flour.
6. Knead on a lightly floured board while adding enough whole wheat flour to make a soft dough.
7. Knead 10 minutes.
8. Form a smooth ball with the dough and place in a large, oiled bowl turning to coat with oil on all sides; cover and rise until doubled.
9. Shape into loaves, put in buttered or oiled bread pans, cover, let rise again, and bake in a preheated 350 degrees F oven for 45-50 minutes, or until the internal temperature of the bread is about 190 degrees F.
10. Loaf will sound hollow when tapped with knuckles on bottom of loaf when done.
11. To avoid having to scald the milk, use non-fat dry milk powder reconstituted according to package directions to make 2 cups.
12. Add an extra tbsp. of butter or vegetable oil to the bread.
13. For a lighter bread, substitute 2 cups unbleached white flour for 2 cups of the rye flour.

German Chocolate Fudge

2 cups semisweet chocolate chips
12 (1 oz.) squares German sweet chocolate
1 (7 oz.) jar marshmallow creme
4 1/2 cups white sugar
2 tbsps. butter
1 (12 fluid oz.) can evaporated milk
1/8 tsp. salt
2 cups chopped pecans

Directions:

1. Combine chocolate chips, German sweet chocolate and marshmallow creme in large bowl.
2. Combine sugar, butter, evaporated milk and salt in heavy skillet.
3. Bring to a boil over medium heat.
4. Cook for 6 minutes, stirring constantly.
5. Pour hot syrup over chocolate mixture.
6. Stir with wooden spoon until smooth. Stir in pecans.
7. Spread into buttered 10x15 inch pan.
8. Let stand until firm; cut into squares.

Krautkrapfen (Bavarian Kraut Crullers)

4 cups all-purpose flour
2 tsps. salt
2 eggs
1/2 cup water
1 pound bacon, cut into small pieces
1 onion, chopped
1 (32 oz.) jar sauerkraut 1 apple, peeled, cored, and chopped
1 cup water 1 cube beef bouillon
2 tsps. salt
1/2 tsp. ground black pepper
2 tsps. butter, cut into small pieces

Directions:

1. In a large bowl, combine flour, salt, eggs and water.
2. Stir until dough has pulled together, then turn it out onto a lightly floured surface and knead until smooth and elastic.
3. If it sticks, add a little oil to your hands.
4. Cover with plastic wrap, and set aside in refrigerator for about 30 minutes.
5. Preheat oven to 350 degrees F (175 degrees C).
6. Place bacon in a skillet over medium heat.
7. Cook until bacon starts to brown. Stir in chopped onion, and cook for about 5 minutes.
8. Stir in sauerkraut, chopped apple, water, bouillon cube, salt and pepper.
9. Reduce heat, cover, and simmer for 15 to 20 minutes.
10. Remove from heat, and let cool.
11. Divide the dough into 2 portions. Lightly oil your work surface, and roll out the dough into thin sheets about 8 by 16 inches.
12. Pour liquid from sauerkraut into a 9x13 inch baking dish, and spread bits of butter into it.
13. Spread kraut mixture evenly over the sheets of dough.
14. Roll sheets up widthwise.
15. Cut slices about 2 inches wide, and place them flat and close together in the baking dish.
16. Bake in preheated oven for 45 minutes, or until dough is lightly browned, and liquid has evaporated.

German Bremer Klaben Holiday Bread

Ingredients:

2 packets active dry yeast
1 cup raisins
1/2 cup warm water
1/2 cup currants
1 1/2 cups milk, lukewarm
3/4 cup slivered almonds
1/2 cup sugar
Grated rind of 3 lemons
1 tsp. salt
1/2 tsp. cardamom
1/2 cup butter, softened
7 1/2 cups sifted flour

Directions:

1. Sprinkle yeast over the warm water.
2. Stir until dissolved. Set aside for 5 minutes.
3. Meanwhile, scald the milk and allow it to cool.
4. Combine lukewarm milk, sugar, salt, butter and about half the flour. Beat for 2 minutes; add the yeast mixture.
5. Toss the nuts and fruit in a small amount of flour to coat. Add this and enough of the remaining flour to the batter to make a soft dough (more or less flour may be needed), along with lemon rind and cardamom.
6. When you have a soft dough, knead on a floured work surface for 10 minutes until smooth and elastic.
7. Place in a buttered bowl, brush top with melted butter, and let rise until doubled in size. Punch down and knead again, form into one long roll, tucking ends under neatly.
8. Place on a greased baking sheet, and let rise until doubled.
9. Bake in a preheated 375 degrees F oven for about 1 hour.
10. Top should be nicely brown. Brush with melted butter or dust with powdered sugar while still warm.

German gingerbread Men Cookies

Ingredients:

1/4 cup boiling water
1/2 cup butter or lard
1/2 cup brown sugar
1/2 cup molasses
3 cups flour
1 tsp. baking soda
1 tsp. salt
1/2 tsp. ginger
1/2 tsp. grated nutmeg
1/8 tsp. cloves

Directions:

1. Pour water over butter or lard and add sugar and molasses.
2. Sift together flour, soda, salt, and spices and beat into sugar mixture.
3. Chill thoroughly.
4. Preheat oven to 375 degrees F.
5. Roll dough thin and cut into shapes with cookie cutter.
6. Bake 8 to 10 minutes.

German Egg Noodles

Ingredients:

4 eggs
1/4 tsp. salt
2 cups flour

Directions:

1. Form any noodle or pasta shape you're familiar with.
2. Beat the eggs using a fork or whisk, just enough to break them up.
3. Add salt, and enough flour to make a stiff dough (more or less than the 2 cups, as needed).
4. On a lightly floured surface, knead the dough until smooth. Long kneading is the secret to good noodles!
5. Cover the noodle dough with plastic wrap or let it rest under a bowl so that it doesn't dry out and the dough can relax. Leave it to rest for 1 hour (if the kitchen is warm, refrigerate the dough).
6. The dough may then be rolled out thinly using a wooden or silicone rolling pin on a lightly floured surface or use a pasta rolling machine.
7. Allow the rolled out dough to dry for 20 to 30 minutes, turning it over when one side is no longer sticky.
8. Roll the dough up, jelly roll fashion, then cut into the desired widths using a sharp knife or pasta roller cutter.
9. To make "Pot Pie Noodles" cut the noodles into 1 1/2 to 2-inch squares. Use to top chicken stew (or a pot-pie filling in a bowl).
10. These noodles may be used in soup, cooked in broth, or serve them as a main dish by bringing a large pot of of salted water to a boil and cook until noodles are tender, but still have a little "bite" (Italians have a word for this - "al dente" or "to the tooth".
11. To serve the ultimate comfort food, the noodles may then be fried in butter with some boiled potatoes and/or garnished with Schmeltz.
12. To make Schmeltz for noodles, melt 1 stick butter in a heavy skillet and stir in 1 cup cream.
13. Alternately, melt 1 stick butter in a heavy skillet and allow to brown. Serve over noodles.
14. Or for a more diet-friendly dish, serve the noodles topped with your favorite tomato-based pasta sauce.
15. This versatile noodle dough can also be used in lasagna, baked with cheese, or as the featured element in a bowl of chicken soup or a beef stew.
16. Or roll out and cut the dough into circles, then fill with a classic ricotta cheese and spinach filling, or stuff with finely chopped, cooked meat to dress up that leftover roast.

German Sweet Potato Pie

Ingredients:

1 2/3 cups cooked mashed (cooled) German sweet potatoes
1 stick butter, melted
1 2/3 cups sugar
3 tbs. flour
2 eggs
1/2 cup milk
1 tbsp. vanilla flavoring

Directions:

1. Preheat oven to 350 degrees F.
2. Mix flour, sugar together.
3. Add butter, milk, eggs and flavoring.
4. Add sweet potatoes.
5. Pour into 2 unbaked pie shells.
6. Bake for about 1 to 1 1/2 hours or until knife comes out clean.

German Chocolate Glazed Peaches

Ingredients:

2 peaches, skinned
1/2 cup sugar
1 box peach gelatin
1 cup of ground cocoa beans type cocoa

Directions:

1. In a bowl mix peaches with some water, sugar, and the gelatin.
2. Soak for an hour or two.
3. Mix the cocoa and add 1 tbsp butter, 1/3 cup of milk, and 1/3 a cup of sugar.
4. Cook together in a pan until it bubbles.
5. Very quickly drain the peaches and glaze.
6. Put these in the freezer for an hour to an hour and a half.

German Chocolate Cherry Cheesecake

Ingredients:

1 box of German chocolate cake mix
1 container cream cheese frosting
1 (8 oz.) pkg. Philadelphia Cream Cheese
1 large can cherry pie filling (or two small)

Directions:

1. Follow direction on box for cake.
2. Mix cream cheese frosting and cream cheese together.
3. Divide the cake mix between 3 round cake pans.
4. Frost first layer with frosting and cherries and repeat until all layers are frosted and have cherries.
5. On top layer, make a design using some cherries.

German Butter Cookies

Ingredients:

1 cup butter
1 cup sugar
1 egg
1 tbsp. milk
1 tsp. vanilla
2 3/4 cups all-purpose flour
1 tsp. baking powder
1/4 tsp. salt

Directions:

1. Cream butter, gradually add sugar and beat until light and fluffy.
2. Beat in egg, milk and vanilla.
3. Combine flour, baking powder and salt.
4. Gradually add to creamed mixture.
5. Chill for ease in handling.
6. Roll out dough to 1/8" thickness on lightly floured surface.
7. Cut with floured cookie cutters into desired shapes.
8. Bake on a cookie sheet in preheated 350 degree F oven 8-10 minutes or until lightly browned.
9. Remove to wire racks to cool.

Almond-Filled Stollen

Ingredients:

1-3/4 cups chopped mixed candied fruit
1/2 cup plus 2 tbsps. rum, divided
2 packages (1/4 oz. each) active dry yeast
1/2 cup warm water (110 degrees F to 115 degrees F)
1-1/2 cups warm milk (110 degrees F to 115 degrees F)
1-1/4 cups butter, softened
2/3 cup sugar
2-1/2 tsps. salt
2 tsps. grated lemon peel
1 tsp. almond extract
7 to 8 cups all-purpose flour
4 eggs
1/3 cup slivered almonds
1 can (8 oz.) almond paste
1 egg yolk
2 tsps. water
2-1/4 cups confectioners' sugar

Directions:

1. In a small bowl, combine candied fruits and 1/2 cup rum; let stand, covered, 1 hour.
2. In a small bowl, dissolve yeast in warm water.
3. In a large bowl, combine milk, butter, sugar, salt, lemon peel, almond extract, remaining rum, yeast mixture and 4 cups flour.
4. Beat on medium speed until smooth. Cover with plastic wrap and let stand in a warm place, about 30 minutes.
5. Beat in eggs.
6. Stir in enough remaining flour to form a soft dough (dough will be sticky). Drain candied fruit, reserving rum for glaze.
7. Reserve 1/2 cup candied fruit for topping. Stir almonds and remaining candied fruit into dough.
8. Turn dough onto a floured surface; knead until smooth and elastic, about 6-8 minutes.
9. Place in a greased bowl, turning once to grease the top.
10. Cover with plastic wrap and let rise in a warm place until doubled, about 1 hour.
11. Punch down dough; divide into three portions.
12. On a greased baking sheet, roll each portion into a 12-in. circle.
13. Crumble one-third of the almond paste over one-half of each circle. Fold dough partially in half, covering filling and placing top layer within 1 in. of bottom edge.

14. Cover with kitchen towels and let rise in a warm place until doubled in size, about 1 hour.
15. Preheat oven to 375 degrees F.
16. In a small bowl, whisk egg yolk and water; brush over loaves.
17. Bake 30-35 minutes or until golden brown.
18. Cover loosely with foil if tops brown too quickly. Remove from pans to wire racks to cool completely.
19. In a small bowl, mix reserved rum with enough confectioner's sugar to make a thin glaze. Drizzle over stollen.
20. Sprinkle with reserved candied fruit.

Prime Rib With Fresh Herb Sauce

Ingredients:

1 bone-in beef rib roast
1 tsp. kosher salt
1 tsp. freshly ground pepper
3 cups water
2 small onions, halved
7 garlic cloves, crushed
5 fresh sage sprigs
5 fresh thyme sprigs
2 bay leaves

Sauce Ingredients:

2 tbsps. butter
2 shallots, thinly sliced
4 garlic cloves, thinly sliced
5 fresh sage sprigs
5 fresh thyme sprigs
2 bay leaves
1 tbsp. all-purpose flour
2 tbsps. cracked black pepper
1/4 tsp. kosher salt
1-1/2 to 2-1/2 cups beef stock, divided
1/2 cup dry red wine or beef stock
1/2 tsp. red wine vinegar
Fresh thyme sprigs, optional

Directions:

1. Preheat oven to 450 degrees F.
2. Place roast in a shallow roasting pan, fat side up; rub with salt and pepper.
3. Add 1 cup water, onions, garlic and herbs to roasting pan. Roast 15 minutes.
4. Reduce oven setting to 325°.
5. Roast 3 to 3-1/2 hours longer or until meat reaches desired doneness (for medium-rare, a thermometer should read 135 degrees F; medium, 140 degrees F; medium-well, 145 degrees F), adding 1 cup water every hour.
6. For sauce, in a large saucepan, heat butter over medium-high heat.
7. Add shallots; cook and stir 5-6 minutes or until tender.
8. Add garlic and herbs; cook 1 minute longer. Stir in flour, pepper and salt until blended.
9. Gradually stir in 1-1/2 cups stock. Remove from heat.

10. Remove roast to a serving platter; tent with foil. Let stand 15 minutes before carving.
11. Meanwhile, strain any pan juices through a sieve into a measuring cup; discard onions and herbs. Skim fat from pan juices.
12. If necessary, add additional stock to pan juices to measure 1 cup.
13. Add to shallot mixture.
14. Place roasting pan over two burners; add wine. Bring to a boil; cook 2-3 minutes, stirring to loosen browned bits from pan. Add to sauce.
15. Bring to a boil, stirring occasionally; cook until mixture is reduced to about 1-1/2 cups, about 10-15 minutes.
16. Stir in vinegar; strain, discarding shallots and herbs. Serve with roast and, if desired, garnish with thyme.

German Mulled Wine

Ingredients:

1 bottle (750 milliliters) fruity red wine
1 cup brandy
1 cup sugar
1 medium orange, sliced
1 medium lemon, sliced
1/8 tsp. ground nutmeg
2 cinnamon sticks (3 inches)
1/2 tsp. whole allspice
1/2 tsp. aniseed
1/2 tsp. whole peppercorns
3 whole cloves
Optional garnishes: orange slices, star anise and additional cinnamon sticks

Directions:

1. In a large saucepan, combine first six ingredients.
2. Place remaining spices on a double thickness of cheesecloth.
3. Gather corners of cloth to enclose spices; tie securely with string.
4. Place in pan.
5. Bring to a boil, stirring occasionally.
6. Reduce heat; simmer gently, covered, 20 minutes.
7. Transfer to a covered container cool slightly.
8. Refrigerate, covered, overnight.
9. Strain wine mixture into a large saucepan, discarding fruit and spice bag; reheat.
10. Serve warm.
11. Garnish as desired.

German Kraut And Keilbasa

Ingredients:

6 keilbasa sausages
32 oz. kraut
4 cups apple cider
1/4 onion cut into rings
4 tbs. brown sugar

Directions:

1. Add all ingredients into a crock pot.
2. Cook 5 hours on High.

German Bratwurst Supper

Ingredients:

3 pounds uncooked bratwurst links
3 pounds small red potatoes, cut into wedges
1 pound baby carrots
1 large red onion, sliced and separated into rings
2 jars (4-1/2 oz. each) whole mushrooms, drained
1/4 cup butter, cubed
1 envelope onion soup mix
2 tbsps. soy sauce
1/2 tsp. pepper

Directions:

1. For each of two foil packets, arrange a double thickness of heavy-duty foil (about 17x15 in.) on a flat surface.
2. Cut brats into thirds.
3. Divide the brats, potatoes, carrots, onion and mushrooms evenly between the two double-layer foil pieces.
4. Dot with butter.
5. Sprinkle with soup mix, soy sauce and pepper.
6. Bring edges of foil together; crimp to seal, forming two large packets.
7. Seal tightly; turn to coat.
8. Grill, covered, over medium heat for 23-28 minutes on each side or until vegetables are tender and sausage is no longer pink.

Slow-Cooked German Sauerkraut Soup

Ingredients:

1 med. potato, cut into 1/4-inch cubes
1 lb. smoked kielbasa, cut into 1/2-inch cubes
1 can (32 oz.) sauerkraut, rinsed and well drained
4 cups chicken broth
1 can (10-3/4 oz.) condensed cream of mushroom soup, undiluted
1/2 pound sliced fresh mushrooms
1 cup cubed cooked chicken
2 medium carrots, sliced
2 celery ribs, sliced
2 tbsps. white vinegar
2 tsps. dill weed
1/2 tsp. pepper
3 to 4 bacon strips, cooked and crumbled

Directions:

1. In a 5-qt. slow cooker, combine the first 12 ingredients.
2. Cover and cook on high for 5-6 hours or until the vegetables are tender.
3. Skim fat.
4. Garnish with bacon.

German Hazelnut Yule Log Cookies

Ingredients:

1 cup butter, softened
3/4 cup packed brown sugar
1 tbsp. lemon juice
1 tsp. grated lemon peel
2-1/2 cups all-purpose flour
1/4 tsp. salt
1-1/2 cups finely chopped hazelnuts
2 tbsps. water

Directions:

1. In a large bowl, cream butter and brown sugar until light and fluffy
2. Beat in lemon juice and peel. In another bowl, mix flour and salt.
3. Gradually beat into creamed mixture.
4. Place hazelnuts in a small bowl.
5. On a lightly floured surface, roll 1/2 cup-fulls of dough into 1/2-in.-thick ropes, about 22 inches long.
6. Cut ropes into 2-in. logs.
7. Lightly brush each log with water; roll in hazelnuts to coat.
8. Place 1 in. apart on ungreased baking sheets.
9. Bake at 375 degrees F for 8-10 minutes or until light brown.
10. Remove to wire racks to cool.

German Potato Dumplings

Ingredients:

3 lbs. medium potatoes, peeled and quartered
1 cup all-purpose flour
3 eggs, lightly beaten
2/3 cup dry bread crumbs
1 tsp. salt
1/2 tsp. ground nutmeg
12 cups water

Browned Butter Sauce Ingredients:

1/2 cup butter, cubed
1 tbsp. chopped onion
1/4 cup dry bread crumbs

Directions:

1. Place potatoes in a Dutch oven; add water to cover.
2. Bring to a boil.
3. Reduce heat; cook, uncovered, 15-20 minutes or until tender.
4. Drain and transfer to a large bowl.
5. Mash potatoes. Stir in flour, eggs, bread crumbs, salt and nutmeg.
6. Shape into sixteen (2-in.) balls.
7. In a Dutch oven, bring 12 cups water to a boil.
8. Carefully add dumplings.
9. Reduce heat; simmer, uncovered, 7-9 minutes or until a toothpick inserted in center of dumplings comes out clean.
10. Meanwhile, in a small heavy saucepan, heat butter and onion over medium heat.
11. Heat 5-7 minutes or until butter is golden brown, stirring constantly.
12. Remove from heat; stir in bread crumbs.
13. Serve with dumplings.

German Lentil Soup

Ingredients:

2 cups dried brown lentils, rinsed and drained
3 cups chicken stock
1 bay leaf
1 cup chopped carrots
1 cup chopped celery
1 cup chopped onion
1 cup cooked, cubed ham
1 tsp. Worcestershire sauce
1/2 tsp. garlic powder
1/4 tsp. freshly grated nutmeg
5 drops hot pepper sauce
1/4 tsp. caraway seed
1/2 tsp. celery salt
1 tbsp. chopped fresh parsley
1/2 tsp. ground black pepper

Directions:

1. Place lentils in a 5 to 6 quart slow cooker.
2. Add chicken stock, bay leaf, carrots, celery, onion, and ham.
3. Season with Worcestershire sauce, garlic powder, nutmeg, hot pepper sauce, caraway seed, celery salt, parsley, and pepper.
4. Cover, and cook on Low for 8 to 10 hours.
5. Remove bay leaf before serving.

Pfannkuchen (German Filled Pancakes)

Ingredients:

1 cup sifted flour
1 1/2 tsp sugar
1/2 tsp salt
1 egg
1 cup milk
1/2 tsp vanilla
3 tbsps. butter
Jam
Sour cream or confectioners' sugar

Directions:

1. Sift together in large bowl the sifted flour, sugar, and salt.
2. Beat the egg, milk and vanilla together in small bowl and add to the flour mixture.
3. Mix thoroughly.
4. Heat the butter/butter in a frying pan over medium heat until it sizzles.
5. Drop the flour mixture by spoonfuls into the pan and fry the pancakes until they are golden brown, turning once.
6. Repeat until all the batter is used, adding more butter to the pan if necessary.
7. The pancakes should be about 4 inches in diameter.
8. Spread the pancakes with your favorite jam and roll them up.
9. Top with sour cream or confectioners' sugar.

Chocolate Lebkuchen (Gingerbread Cookies)

Ingredients:

1 cup plus 2 tbsps. all-purpose flour
1/4 cup sugar
Dash salt
1/3 cup cold butter, cubed
3 tbsps. water
1 tsp. vanilla extract

Topping Ingredients:

1/4 cup butter, softened
1/4 cup sugar
1 large egg
1 tbsp. canola oil
2/3 cup quick-cooking oats
1/2 cup all-purpose flour
1/3 cup ground almonds
1/3 cup ground hazelnuts
1/4 cup baking cocoa
1 tsp. baking powder
1/2 tsp. ground cinnamon
1/4 tsp. each ground cloves, cardamom and allspice
1/4 cup finely chopped candied lemon peel
1/4 cup finely chopped candied orange peel

Glaze Ingredients:

6 oz. semisweet chocolate, chopped
2 oz. unsweetened chocolate, chopped
1/4 cup butter, cubed

Directions:

1. In a small bowl, combine the flour, sugar and salt; cut in butter until mixture resembles coarse crumbs.
2. Combine water and vanilla; gradually add to crumb mixture, tossing with a fork until dough forms a ball.
3. On a lightly floured surface, roll out dough to 1/16-in. thickness.
4. Cut with a floured 2-1/2-in. round cookie cutter.
5. Place on ungreased baking sheets.
6. Bake at 325 degrees F for 8-10 minutes or until set.
7. Remove from pans to wire racks to cool.
8. For topping, in a small bowl, cream butter and sugar until light and fluffy. Beat in egg and oil.

9. Combine the oats, flour, nuts, cocoa, baking powder and spices; gradually add to creamed mixture and mix well.
10. Fold in candied peels.
11. Drop a rounded tablespoonful of topping on each cookie; gently press down.
12. Place 2 in. apart on ungreased baking sheets. Bake at 325 degrees F for 13-16 minutes or until set.
13. Remove from pans to wire racks to cool.
14. In a microwave-safe bowl, melt chocolate and butter; stir until smooth.
15. Dip each cookie halfway in chocolate; allow excess to drip off.
16. Place on waxed paper; let stand until set.

Gingerbread Men Cookies

Ingredients:

1/2 cup butter, softened
3/4 cup packed dark brown sugar
1/3 cup molasses
1 large egg
2 tbsps. water
2-2/3 cups all-purpose flour
1 tsp. baking soda
1/2 tsp. salt
2 tsps. ground ginger
1/2 tsp. ground cinnamon
1/2 tsp. ground nutmeg
1/2 tsp. ground allspice
Frosting of choice

Directions:

1. Cream butter and brown sugar until light and fluffy.
2. Beat in molasses, egg and water. In another bowl, whisk together remaining ingredients minus frosting.
3. Gradually beat into creamed mixture.
4. Divide dough in half. Shape each into a disk; wrap in plastic.
5. Refrigerate until easy to handle, about 30 minutes.
6. Preheat oven to 350 degrees F.
7. On a lightly floured surface, roll each portion of dough to 1/8-in. thickness.
8. Cut with a floured 4-in. gingerbread man cookie cutter.
9. Place 2 in. apart on greased baking sheets.
10. Bake until edges are firm, 8-10 minutes.
11. Remove to wire racks to cool completely.
12. Frost as desired.

German Eggnog

Ingredients:

8 cups milk, divided
6 large eggs
1 cup plus
2 tbsps. sugar, divided
1/2 cup rum
1/2 cup brandy
1/2 tsp. ground nutmeg
3 cups heavy whipping cream
Cinnamon sticks and additional ground nutmeg

Directions:

1. In a large saucepan, heat 4 cups milk until bubbles form around sides of pan.
2. Meanwhile, in a large bowl, whisk eggs and 1 cup sugar until blended. Slowly stir in hot milk; return all to saucepan.
3. Cook over medium-low heat 6-8 minutes or until slightly thickened and a thermometer reads at least 160 degrees F, stirring constantly (do not allow to boil). Immediately transfer to a large bowl.
4. Stir in rum, brandy, nutmeg and remaining milk.
5. Refrigerate, covered, several hours or until cold.
6. In a large bowl, beat cream until it begins to thicken.
7. Add remaining sugar; beat until soft peaks form.
8. Fold into egg mixture. (Mixture may separate; stir before serving.)
9. If desired, serve with cinnamon sticks and additional nutmeg.

German Red Cabbage

Ingredients:

1 medium onion, halved and sliced
1 medium apple, sliced
1 head red cabbage, shredded (8 cups)
1/3 cup sugar
1/3 cup white vinegar
3/4 tsp. salt, optional
1/4 tsp. pepper

Directions:

1. In a large Dutch oven coated with cooking spray, cook and stir onion and apple over medium heat until onion is tender, about 5 minutes.
2. Stir in remaining ingredients.
3. Cook, covered, until cabbage is tender, about 1 hour, stirring occasionally.
4. Serve warm or cold.

German Snow Angel Cookies

Ingredients:

1 cup butter, softened
1 cup granulated sugar
1-1/2 tsps. vanilla extract
2 large eggs
3-1/2 cups all-purpose flour
1 tsp. ground cinnamon
1/2 tsp. baking powder
1/2 tsp. salt
1/4 tsp. ground nutmeg
1/4 tsp. ground cloves

Frosting Ingredients:

9 cups confectioners' sugar
3/4 cup shortening
1/2 cup lemon juice
4 to 6 tbsps. water
Coarse sugar, optional

Directions:

1. In a large bowl, beat butter, sugar and vanilla until blended.
2. Beat in eggs, one at a time. In another bowl, whisk flour, cinnamon, baking powder, salt, nutmeg and cloves; gradually beat into creamed mixture.
3. Divide dough in half. Shape each into a disk.
4. Wrap in plastic.
5. Refrigerate 1 hour or until firm enough to roll.
6. Preheat oven to 350 degrees F.
7. On a lightly floured surface, roll each portion of dough to 1/8-in. thickness. Cut with a floured 4-in. angel-shaped cookie cutter.
8. Place 1 in. apart on ungreased baking sheets.
9. Bake 12-14 minutes or until edges begin to brown.
10. Remove from pans to wire racks to cool completely.
11. For frosting, in a large bowl, beat confectioners' sugar, shortening, lemon juice and enough water to reach a spreading consistency.
12. Spread or pipe over cookies.
13. Sprinkle with coarse sugar.

Pork Schnitzel With Dill Sauce

Ingredients:

1/2 cup all-purpose flour
2 tsps. seasoned salt
1/2 tsp. pepper
2 large eggs
1/4 cup 2% milk
1-1/2 cups dry bread crumbs
2 tsps. paprika
6 pork sirloin cutlets (4 oz. each)
6 tbsps. canola oil

Dill Sauce Ingredients:

2 tbsps. all-purpose flour
1-1/2 cups chicken broth, divided
1 cup (8 oz.) sour cream
1/2 tsp. dill weed

Directions:

1. In a shallow bowl, mix flour, seasoned salt and pepper. In a second shallow bowl, whisk eggs and milk until blended. In a third bowl, mix bread crumbs and paprika.
2. Pound pork cutlets with a meat mallet to 1/4-in. thickness.
3. Dip cutlets in flour mixture to coat both sides; shake off excess.
4. Dip in egg mixture, then in crumb mixture, patting to help coating adhere.
5. In a large skillet, heat oil over medium heat.
6. Add pork in batches; cook 2-3 minutes on each side or until golden brown.
7. Remove to a serving plate; keep warm. Wipe skillet clean if necessary.
8. In a small bowl, whisk flour and broth until smooth.
9. Add to same skillet.
10. Bring to a boil, stirring constantly; cook and stir 2 minutes or until thickened.
11. Reduce heat to low.
12. Stir in sour cream and dill; heat through (do not boil).
13. Serve with pork.

German Parmesan Baked Potatoes

6 tbsps. butter, melted
3 tbsps. grated Parmesan cheese
8 med. unpeeled red potatoes (2-3/4 pounds), halved lengthwise

Directions:

1. Pour butter into a 13-in. x 9-in. baking pan.
2. Sprinkle Parmesan cheese over butter.
3. Place potatoes with cut sides down over cheese.
4. Bake, uncovered, at 400 degrees F for 40-45 minutes or until tender.

German Cranberry Conserve

Ingredients:

4 cups fresh or frozen cranberries, halved
1 tbsp. grated orange peel
2 oranges, peeled, sliced and quartered
1 cup raisins
1-1/4 cup water
1 cup chopped pecans
2-1/2 cups sugar

Directions:

1. In a large saucepan, combine the cranberries, orange peel, oranges, raisins and water.
2. Cover and simmer over medium heat until cranberries are soft.
3. Add pecans and sugar; stir well.
4. Simmer, uncovered, 10-15 minutes, stirring often.
5. Cool.
6. Spoon into covered containers.
7. Refrigerate.
8. Serve as a relish with poultry or pork, or spread on biscuits or rolls.

German Sauerkraut Casserole

Ingredients:

1 lb. mild Italian sausage links, cut into 1-inch slices
1 large onion, chopped
2 apples, peeled and quartered
1 can (27 oz.) sauerkraut, undrained
1 cup water
1/2 cup packed brown sugar
2 tsps. caraway seed
Snipped parsley, optional

Directions:

1. In a skillet, cook sausage and onion until sausage is brown and onion is tender; drain.
2. Stir in apples, sauerkraut, water, brown sugar and caraway seed.
3. Transfer to a 2-1/2-qt. baking dish.
4. Cover and bake at 350 degrees F for 1 hour.
5. Garnish with parsley if desired.

Bavarian Pot Roast

Ingredients:

1 boneless beef chuck pot roast
2 tbsps. canola oil
1-1/4 cups water
3/4 cup beer or beef broth
1 can (8 oz.) tomato sauce
1/2 cup chopped onion
2 tbsps. sugar
1 tbsp. vinegar
2 tsps. salt
1 tsp. ground cinnamon
1 bay leaf
1/2 tsp. pepper
1/2 tsp. ground ginger
Cornstarch and water, optional

Directions:

1. In a Dutch oven, brown roast in hot oil.
2. Combine water, beer, tomato sauce, onion, sugar, vinegar, salt, cinnamon, bay leaf, pepper and ginger.
3. Pour over meat and bring to a boil.
4. Reduce heat; cover and simmer until meat is tender, about 2-1/2-3 hours.
5. Remove meat.
6. Discard bay leaf. If desired, thicken juices with cornstarch and water.

Roast Christmas Goose

Ingredients:

1 goose (10 to 12 lbs.)
Salt and pepper
1 med. apple, peeled and quartered
1 med. navel orange, peeled and quartered
1 med. lemon, peeled and quartered
1 cup hot water

Directions:

1. Sprinkle the goose cavity with salt and pepper.
2. Place apple, orange and lemon in the cavity.
3. Place breast side up on a rack in a large shallow roasting pan.
4. Prick skin well with a fork.
5. Pour water into pan.
6. Bake, uncovered, at 350 degrees F for 2-1/4 to 2-3/5 hours or until a meat thermometer reads 185 degrees F.
7. If necessary, drain fat from pan as it accumulates.
8. Discard fruit.
9. Serve and enjoy!

Zimtsterne

Ingredients:

1 cup butter, softened
2 cups sugar
2 eggs
3 oz. semisweet chocolate, melted and cooled
2-3/4 cups all-purpose flour
1/3 cup ground cinnamon

Directions:

1. In a large bowl, cream butter and sugar until light and fluffy.
2. Beat in eggs and chocolate.
3. Combine flour and cinnamon; gradually add to creamed mixture and mix well.
4. Wrap dough in plastic wrap; refrigerate for 1 hour or until easy to handle.
5. On a lightly floured surface, roll out dough to 1/4-in. thickness.
6. Cut with a floured 2-in. star-shaped cookie cutter.
7. Place 1 in. apart on ungreased baking sheets.
8. Chill and reroll scraps if desired.
9. Bake at 350 degrees F for 9-11 minutes or until edges are firm.
10. Remove to wire racks.

Pfeffernuesse Cookies

Ingredients:

1/2 cup molasses
1/4 cup honey
1/4 cup butter, cubed
1/4 cup shortening
2 large eggs
1 1/2 tsps. anise extract
4 cups all-purpose flour
3/4 cup sugar
1/2 cup packed brown sugar
2 tsps. ground cinnamon
1-1/2 tsps. baking soda
1 tsp. ground ginger
1 tsp. ground cardamom
1 tsp. ground nutmeg
1 tsp. ground cloves
3/4 tsp. coarsely ground pepper
1/2 tsp. salt
1 cup confectioners' sugar

Directions:

1. In a small saucepan, combine molasses, honey, butter and shortening.
2. Cook and stir over medium heat until melted. Remove from heat; cool to room temperature.
3. Stir in eggs and extract.
4. Combine flour, sugar, brown sugar, cinnamon, baking soda, ginger, cardamom, nutmeg, cloves, pepper and salt.
5. Gradually add molasses mixture and mix well.
6. Cover and refrigerate at least 2 hours or overnight.
7. Preheat oven to 325 degrees F. Roll dough into 1-in. balls.
8. Place 1 in. apart on greased baking sheets. Bake 12-15 minutes or until golden brown.
9. Remove cookies to wire racks.
10. Roll warm cookies in confectioners' sugar.
11. Cool completely.

German Potato Dumplings

Ingredients:

2 day-old hard rolls
1/2 cup water
2 tsps. canola oil
1/2 cup leftover mashed potatoes
1 egg, lightly beaten
Dash ground nutmeg
1 to 2 tbsps. all-purpose flour
1/4 cup butter, cubed

Directions:

1. Tear rolls into 1/2-in. pieces; place in a 15-in. x 10-in. x 1-in. baking pan.
2. Drizzle with water and squeeze dry.
3. In a large skillet, heat oil over medium-high. Add bread; cook and stir for 1-2 minutes or until lightly toasted.
4. In a small bowl, combine the potatoes, egg, nutmeg and bread.
5. Add enough flour to achieve desired consistency to shape into balls.
6. With floured hands, shape mixture into 3-in. balls.
7. Fill a Dutch oven two-thirds full with water; bring to a boil.
8. Carefully add dumplings.
9. Reduce heat; simmer, uncovered, for 8-10 minutes or until a toothpick inserted into a dumpling comes out clean.
10. Meanwhile, in a heavy saucepan, heat butter over medium heat until golden brown. Serve dumplings warm with butter.

Kummelweck Rolls

Ingredients:

3 1/4 cups all-purpose flour, divided
1 cup warm water (105 degrees F/41 degrees C)
1 (.25 oz.) package active dry yeast
2 1/2 tbsps. vegetable oil, divided
1 large egg white
1 tbsp. sugar
1 1/2 tsps. salt
1 tsp. honey, or more to taste

Topping Ingredients:

1 large egg white
2 tsps. water
1/2 tsp. caraway seeds, or to taste
Sea salt to taste

Directions:

1. Whisk 1/2 cup flour, 1 cup warm water, and yeast together in the bowl of a stand mixer. Let sit until foamy, 10 to 15 minutes.
2. Stir 2 tbsps. oil, 1 egg white, sugar, salt, and honey into yeast mixture; whisk until smooth.
3. Gradually add flour to yeast mixture while mixer is running with the dough hook attached; knead until a soft, sticky dough forms, 3 to 4 minutes.
4. Drizzle remaining vegetable oil into the bowl and turn dough to coat.
5. Cover the bowl and let dough rise until doubled in size, 1 to 2 hours.
6. Line a baking sheet with a silicone baking mat.
7. Turn dough out onto a lightly floured work surface, flatten dough, and press into rectangle. Cut dough into 12 pieces and form pieces into rolls.
8. Place rolls 2-inches apart on prepared baking sheet. Cover and let rise until doubled in size, about 30 minutes.
9. Preheat oven to 425 degrees F (220 degrees C).
10. Whisk 1 egg white and 2 tsps. water together in a small bowl.
11. Use kitchen shears to cut an X at the top of each roll. Brush rolls with egg white mixture and sprinkle with caraway seeds and salt.
12. Bake in the preheated oven until golden brown, 18 to 20 minutes.

Hasenpfeffer (Rabbit Stew)

3 pounds rabbit meat, cleaned and cut into pieces
1/2 tsp. salt
1/3 cup all-purpose flour
1/2 lb. bacon, diced
1/2 cup finely chopped shallots
1 clove garlic, finely chopped
1 cup dry red wine
1 cup water
1 tbsp. chicken bouillon granules
1 tbsp. currant jelly
10 black peppercorns, crushed
1 bay leaf
1/4 tsp. dried rosemary, crushed
2 tsps. lemon juice
3 tbsps. water
2 tbsps. all-purpose flour
1/8 tsp. dried thyme, crushed

Directions:

1. Place bacon in a large, deep skillet.
2. Cook over medium high heat until evenly brown.
3. Drain on paper towels and set aside.
4. Sprinkle rabbit with salt and coat with 1/3 cup flour, shaking off excess.
5. Brown rabbit in remaining bacon fat.
6. Remove from skillet, along with all but 2 tbsps. of the fat, and reserve.
7. Sauté shallots and garlic in skillet for about 4 minutes, until tender. Stir in wine, 1 cup water and bouillon. Heat to boiling, then stir in jelly, peppercorns, bay leaf, and rosemary.
8. Return rabbit and bacon to skillet.
9. Heat to boiling, then reduce heat to low.
10. Cover and let simmer about 1 1/2 hours or until rabbit is tender.
11. Remove bay leaf and discard. Place rabbit on a warm platter and keep warm while preparing gravy.
12. To Make Gravy: Stir lemon juice into skillet with cooking liquid. Combine 3 tbsps. water with 2 tbsps. flour and mix together; stir mixture into skillet over low heat.
13. Finally, stir in thyme.
14. Pour gravy over stew and serve, or pour into a gravy boat and serve on the side.

German Potato Plum Dumplings

Ingredients:

4 large russet potatoes
1/2 tsp. salt
1 tbsp. butter, softened
2 eggs, beaten
1/4 cup farina
1 cup all-purpose flour, or as needed
12 Italian prune plums
12 cubes white sugar
1/2 cup butter, melted
1/4 cup white sugar
1 cup dry bread crumbs
Additional melted butter and sugar for garnish

Directions:

1. Scrub potatoes, and place them into a large pot with enough water to cover.
2. Bring to a boil, and cook until tender, about 40 minutes.
3. Drain, and cool.
4. When potatoes are cool enough to handle, peel, and press through a ricer into a large bowl. Set aside to cool.
5. This part of the process can be done as much as one day in advance.
6. In a large bowl, mix together the prepared potatoes, salt, egg, and 1 tbsp. of butter until well blended.
7. Gradually stir in the farina, and then the flour. If dough is still wet, more flour can be mixed in.
8. Turn dough out onto a floured surface, and knead until smooth, about 5 to 10 minutes.
9. Split open each plum where it cracks, and remove the pit. Replace each pit with a sugar cube, and close.
10. On a floured surface, roll out the dough to 1/4 inch thickness.
11. Cut into twelve 3 inch squares.
12. Place one plum into each square, and bring the corners around to the top.
13. Pinch together all of the seams to seal.
14. Bring a large pot of water to a slow boil. Place about 4 dumplings into the water at a time.
15. Once they float to the surface, continue to cook them for about 5 more minutes. Transfer cooked dumplings to a covered bowl, and keep warm.
16. Melt the remaining 1/2 cup of butter in a small skillet over medium heat.

17. Stir in bread crumbs, and 1/4 cup of sugar.
18. Continue to cook and stir until browned.
19. Remove the bread crumbs to a plate, and roll warm dumplings in the mixture until entirely coated.
20. To serve, place a dumpling or two on a plate, sprinkle with a little sugar and a little extra melted butter, if desired.

Angel's Braid (Engelszopf)

Ingredients:

1.8 oz. golden raisins
4 tbsps. Kirschwasser distilled German cherry brandy
5 1/3 cups flour
1 cube fresh yeast or 1 package dry yeast
1/3 cup brown sugar or turbinado sugar
4.5 oz. each of sour cream and heavy cream
7 tbsps. unsalted butter
2 eggs
1.8 oz. chopped almonds
1.8 oz. diced candied orange peel
3 tbsps. unsweetened grated coconut
Flour for the work surface
1 egg yolk
1 tbsp. milk
3 tbsps. almond slivers

Directions:

1. Soak the raisins in Kirschwasser.
2. Sift the flour into a bowl and make an indentation in the middle.
3. Add the yeast (crumble the fresh yeast) and sprinkle with 1 tsp. sugar.
4. Combine the sour cream and heavy cream, warm up about 1/4 of the mixture, combine it with the yeast and sprinkle with a bit of flour.
5. Let everything rest at a warm spot for about 30 minutes.
6. Add the remaining sugar, soft butter and eggs, and knead everything into a dough. Then add the soaked raisins, almonds, candied orange peel and grated coconut, and let everything rest for another 30-60 minutes.
7. Dust the work surface lightly with flour and knead the dough, and divide it into three parts.
8. Form three logs and braid them together.
9. Cover the braid and let it rest for another 45 minutes.
10. Preheat the oven to 350°F (180°C)
11. Mix the egg yolks and milk, spread over the mixture over the braid and sprinkle with the almond slivers.
12. Bake in the hot oven until golden for 30-40 minutes.

Christmas Gingerbread House

Ingredients:

12 tbsps. unsalted German butter softened, 1-1/2 sticks
1-1/2 cups light brown sugar
2 large eggs
1 cup dark molasses
1 tbsp. fresh orange juice
6 cups all-purpose flour
1/2 tsp. baking powder
4 tsps. ground ginger
3 tsps. ground cinnamon
1/2 tsp.
Salt
2-2/3 cups confectioner's sugar
2 tbsps. powdered egg white
1/4 cup water
Assorted German cookies and candies

Directions:

1. Beat together flour and sugar until light and fluffy.
2. Add eggs one at a time, beating after each addition.
3. Beat in molasses and orange juice. Stir together flour, baking powder, ginger, cinnamon and salt in a separate bowl, and add half of this dry mixture to molasses mixture, beating until smooth.
4. Add remaining flour and beat until it comes together; knead by hand until completely smooth and workable. Wrap dough tightly in plastic and let rest in a cool place (but not the refrigerator) for an hour or two.
5. Meanwhile, cut out patterns using lightweight cardboard.
6. For the roof, cut two 6 1/2by 7-inch rectangles.
7. For the front and back, cut two 12-inch high by 5 1/2-inches wide rectangles; to create a triangle at the top, fold the sides until they meet exactly in the middle of the top, 2 3/4 inches in, and cut along the fold marks.
8. For the sides, cut two 7 1/2-inch high by 5-inch rectangles.
9. Preheat oven to 350 degrees F. Divide gingerbread dough in half; cover one half with plastic, and place other half on a large sheet of parchment paper.
10. On the paper, roll dough to 1/4 inch thickness.
11. Rub dough surface very lightly with flour, and place any many patterns on dough as will fit.
12. Use a sharp knife to cut them out.

13. Use paper underneath to transfer them to baking sheets, cutting it away from other pieces as necessary. Re-roll dough as necessary, though work quickly to keep it moist.
14. If desired, cut a skylight into one of the roof pieces.
15. Press a rectangle "door" cookie on front piece, and a larger rectangle "garage" cookie on back piece.
16. Cut out windows as desired on front, side and back pieces.
17. Bake pieces just until sides begin to darken, 10 to 15 minutes.
18. To put house together, it's helpful to have two people.
19. Prop up the front and a side, and use stiff icing to seal (stiff icing recipe below).
20. Repeat with back and other side, and then seal the two pieces together.
21. Assemble inverted v-shape roof by itself, and then attach it to house.
22. If it's not important that the house be edible, it's an easy alternative to construct a house first out of the cardboard pattern pieces, using heavyweight tape to attach them, and then glue the gingerbread pieces over it.
23. Place the house on a piece of foil-covered heavyweight cardboard, and decorate from there, using stiff icing to attach candies and cookies as shingles, roof decorations, trim, stepping stones, bushes, and perhaps a driveway and some garden adornments.
24. Beat together 2 2/3 cups confectioners sugar, 2 tbsps. powdered egg white and 1/4 cup water until stiff.
25. Cover tightly and store up to two weeks; this dries to be very firm and makes a good "glue" for gingerbread houses

About the Author

Laura Sommers is **The Recipe Lady!**

She is a loving wife and mother who lives on a small farm in Baltimore County, Maryland and has a passion for all things domestic especially when it comes to saving money. She has a profitable eBay business and is a couponing addict. Follow her tips and tricks to learn how to make delicious meals on a budget, save money or to learn the latest life hack!

Visit her Amazon Author Page to see her latest books:

amazon.com/author/laurasommers

Visit the Recipe Lady's blog for even more great recipes:

http://the-recipe-lady.blogspot.com/

Follow the Recipe Lady on **Pinterest**:

http://pinterest.com/therecipelady1

Laura Sommers is also an Extreme Couponer and Penny Hauler! If you would like to find out how to get things for **FREE** with coupons or how to get things for only a **PENNY**, then visit her couponing blog
Penny Items and Freebies

http://penny-items-and-freebies.blogspot.com/

Other Books by Laura Sommers

- **Christmas Stuffing Recipes**
- **Christmas Hot Chocolate Recipes**
- **Christmas Cookies**
- **Candy Corn Cookbook**
- **Halloween Recipes**
- **50 Pumpkin Recipes**
- **Recipes for Leftover Thanksgiving or Christmas Turkey**

May all of your meals be a banquet
with good friends and good food.

Printed in Great Britain
by Amazon